Copyright © 2025 by Immortal Ink Publishing

Book design by Lucero Rabaudi

All rights reserved,
Published in the United States by Immortal Ink Publishing Santa Barbara, CA.

Immortalinkpublishing.shop

Library of Congress Cataloging-in-Publication Data is available.

ISBN 979-8-218-65851-9

Printed in the United States of America

A Father's Journey was born from deep admiration and reflection. Growing up without a consistent father figure shaped the way I saw the world—and shaped what I longed to understand more deeply. This journal was created as a space for fathers to look back on their lives, their relationships with their own parents, and the path they've carved through the joys and challenges of fatherhood.

The inspiration behind this book is from my brother Justin—a man who became an incredible father without ever having a true role model to guide him. Watching him parent with love, strength, and intention has been one of the most moving things I've witnessed. He reminded me that we are not limited by the examples we had, but are capable of creating new legacies.

I hope this journal offers a place for fathers to reflect, to remember, and to pass on something meaningful. This is more than a book—it's a keepsake for generations.

add photo here

BIRTH

Full name at birth:_____

Date of birth:_____

Height/Weight:_____

Place of birth:_____

Parents names:_____

Meaning of name:_____

President:_____

Average price for a home:_____

Average annual income:_____

Gallon of gas:_____

Gallon of milk:_____

Dozen eggs:_____

INFANT

My siblings and their birthdays:_____
_____
_____
_____
_____
_____

This is how my parents described me as a baby:
_____
_____
_____
_____
_____
_____
_____
_____
_____

TODDLER

I first learned to walk:_____

_____

_____

_____

_____

My first words were :_____

_____

_____

_____

_____

When I quit wearing diapers:_____

_____

_____

_____

_____

When I first learned to count:_____

_____

_____

CHILDHOOD

Nickname:_____

_____

_____

I grew up in: _____

_____

_____

_____

My best friend/s from childhood was:

_____

_____

_____

_____

_____

_____

_____

CHILDHOOD

My favorite childhood memory:

_____
_____
_____
_____
_____
_____
_____
_____
_____
_____
_____
_____
_____
_____
_____
_____
_____

CHILDHOOD

I miss this most about my childhood:

_____

_____

_____

_____

_____

_____

_____

_____

_____

_____

_____

_____

_____

_____

_____

CHILDHOOD

Add photos here

CHILDHOOD

Add photos here

CHILDHOOD

Add photos here

CHILDHOOD

Some of my favorite TV shows were:

_____
_____
_____
_____

Some of my favorite toys were:

_____
_____
_____
_____
_____
_____

My favorite songs were:

_____
_____
_____
_____
_____

CHILDHOOD

I played these sources:

_____
_____
_____
_____

This was the first sporting event I went to:

_____
_____
_____
_____
_____
_____
_____
_____
_____
_____
_____
_____

CHILDHOOD

This is who I looked up to most and why:

_____

_____

_____

_____

_____

_____

_____

_____

_____

_____

_____

_____

_____

_____

_____

_____

CHILDHOOD

Some of my favorite foods, candys, drinks ect were:

_____
_____
_____
_____
_____

I started to cook at this age.. and this is what I cooked first:

_____
_____
_____
_____
_____
_____
_____
_____
_____
_____

CHILDHOOD

This is what my parents would prepare for meals:

_____
_____
_____
_____
_____
_____
_____
_____
_____
_____
_____
_____
_____
_____
_____
_____

CHILDHOOD

How I spent my summers:

CHILDHOOD

Favorite memory with Grandparents:

___

ADOLESCENCE

This is how I dressed and styled my hair:

ADOLESCENCE

Add photos here

ADOLESCENCE

Add photos here

ADOLESCENCE

My favorite bands/artists were:

___

ADOLESCENCE

My first concert ever was:

ADOLESCENCE

These are the sports I played:

ADOLESCENCE

My hobbies were:

_____

_____

_____

_____

_____

_____

_____

_____

_____

_____

_____

_____

_____

_____

ADOLESCENCE

This is how I spent my weekends:

_____

_____

_____

_____

_____

_____

_____

_____

_____

_____

_____

_____

_____

_____

_____

ADOLESCENCE

These were all my friends:

_____
_____
_____
_____
_____
_____
_____
_____
_____
_____
_____
_____
_____
_____
_____
_____
_____
_____

ADOLESCENCE

My dating life in highschool:

_____
_____
_____
_____
_____
_____
_____
_____
_____
_____
_____
_____
_____
_____
_____
_____
_____

ADOLESCENCE

I went to prom with:

_____

_____

_____

_____

_____

_____

_____

_____

_____

_____

_____

_____

_____

_____

_____

_____

ADOLESCENCE

I learned to drive when:

ADOLESCENCE

My very first car was:

___
___
___
___
___
___
___
___

My dream car at the time was:

___
___
___
___
___
___
___

ADOLESCENCE

These are the kinds of grades I got:

_____
_____
_____
_____

My most and least favorite subjects :

_____
_____
_____
_____
_____
_____
_____
_____
_____
_____

ADOLESCENCE

My favorite teachers:

ADOLESCENCE

This was my very first job and this is how much I made:

ADOLESCENCE

This was my dream job:

ADOLESCENCE

This was my highschool and the year I graduated:

The advice I would give my teenage self now, and what I would change:

FAMILY

My Mother's maiden name was:

_____

My relationship with my Mother was like this:

_____

_____

_____

_____

_____

_____

_____

_____

_____

_____

_____

_____

_____

FAMILY

My relationship with my Father was like this:

_____

_____

_____

_____

_____

_____

_____

_____

_____

_____

_____

_____

_____

_____

_____

_____

FAMILY

Add photos here

FAMILY

Add photos here

FAMILY

This is how my parents met:

FAMILY

My relationship with my siblings was like this:

FAMILY

This is how I'm similar and different from my family:

FAMILY

These are the unique gifts and talents that my parents had:

FAMILY

Family traditions that were passed to me:

FAMILY

The best advice my parents gave me:

_____

_____

_____

_____

_____

_____

_____

_____

_____

_____

_____

_____

_____

_____

_____

_____

FAMILY

What I do better than anyone else in my family:

___

FAMILY

My favorite memory of my Mother:

_____

_____

_____

_____

_____

_____

_____

_____

_____

_____

_____

_____

_____

_____

_____

FAMILY

My favorite memory of my Father:

FAMILY

The best advice my Grandparents gave me:

_____

_____

_____

_____

_____

_____

_____

_____

_____

_____

_____

_____

_____

_____

_____

_____

_____

FATHERHOOD

My first reaction when I found out I was going to be a Father:

_____

_____

_____

This is how old I was and what it was like when I became a Father:

_____

_____

_____

_____

_____

_____

_____

_____

The name I wanted for my child other than the one chosen:

_____

_____

FATHERHOOD

Add photos here

FATHERHOOD

Add photos here

FATHERHOOD

My baby's first words:

_____
_____
_____
_____

When they first learned to walk:

_____
_____
_____
_____

This is what I had to do to calm them:

_____
_____
_____
_____
_____
_____
_____

FATHERHOOD

The ways my child/children are similar/different than me:

___

___

___

___

___

___

___

___

___

___

___

___

___

___

___

___

___

___

___

___

FATHERHOOD

A time my child/children made me proud:

_____

_____

_____

_____

_____

_____

_____

_____

_____

_____

_____

_____

_____

_____

_____

_____

FATHERHOOD

The most rewarding/challenging parts of fatherhood:

_____
_____
_____
_____
_____
_____
_____
_____
_____
_____
_____
_____
_____
_____
_____
_____
_____
_____
_____

FATHERHOOD

My hopes and dreams for my child/children:

_____

_____

_____

_____

_____

_____

_____

_____

_____

_____

_____

_____

_____

_____

_____

_____

FATHERHOOD

The things I would change about how my child/children were raised:

___

___

___

___

___

___

___

___

___

___

___

___

___

___

___

___

___

___

SPIRITUALITY

The beliefs or religious practices of my parents when I was growing up:

SPIRITUALITY

How my beliefs and religious practices have changed throughout life:

SPIRITUALITY

Fate? Or free will? This is what I believe has the most influence:

___

SPIRITUALITY

I believe the purpose of life is:

SPIRITUALITY

Miracles and my personal beliefs about them:

SPIRITUALITY

This person has had the biggest spiritual influence on my life:

CAREER

My career/s throughout life and where the inspiration came from:

_____
_____
_____
_____
_____
_____
_____
_____
_____
_____
_____
_____
_____
_____
_____
_____
_____
_____
_____

CAREER

The business I've always wanted to have:

_____
_____
_____
_____

If I could have any profession in life, it would be this:

_____
_____
_____
_____
_____
_____
_____

The profession my parents wanted for me:

_____
_____
_____
_____

CAREER

Add photos here

CAREER

Add photos here

TRAVEL

This is my favorite place to visit:

___

My dream destination:

___

TRAVEL

My favorite travel memory:

_____
_____
_____
_____
_____
_____
_____
_____
_____
_____
_____
_____
_____
_____
_____
_____
_____
_____
_____
_____
_____

TRAVEL

Add photos here

TRAVEL

Add photos here

TRAVEL

The top ten places I would like to visit and why:

LOVE

My beliefs on soulmates:

_____
_____
_____
_____
_____
_____
_____
_____
_____
_____
_____
_____
_____
_____
_____
_____
_____

LOVE

The most important qualities in a successful relationship:

LOVE

Add photos here

LOVE

Add photos here

LOVE

The biggest way I believe relationships have changed over the years:

___

Love poem or song written/ dedicated to me:

___

LOVE

Advice I would share with new couples:

SELF

My daily routine, workout, diet, ect.:

_____
_____
_____
_____
_____
_____
_____
_____
_____
_____
_____
_____
_____
_____
_____
_____
_____

SELF

My introversion/extroversion and how that's changed throughout life:

_____
_____
_____
_____
_____
_____
_____
_____
_____
_____
_____
_____
_____
_____
_____
_____
_____

SELF

Add photos here

SELF

Add photos here

SELF

What I love most about myself:

SELF

The most impulsive thing I've ever done:

SELF

Some of my favorite foods now:

_____
_____
_____
_____
_____
_____

My favorite seasons:

_____
_____
_____
_____
_____
_____
_____
_____

SELF

My favorite holidays and why:

___

SELF

My most cherished holiday memory:

___

___

___

___

___

___

___

___

___

___

___

___

___

___

___

___

___

___

___

___

___

SELF

I'm most proud of these accomplishments:

_____
_____
_____
_____
_____
_____
_____
_____
_____
_____
_____
_____
_____
_____
_____

SELF

A perfect day for me would look like this:

_____
_____
_____
_____
_____
_____
_____
_____
_____
_____
_____
_____
_____
_____
_____
_____
_____
_____

SELF

My top ten favorite movies, TV shows, and books:

SELF

My favorite band/artist and how that's changed over my life:

SELF

If I got to start all over at life, this is what I would change:

_____
_____
_____
_____
_____
_____
_____
_____
_____
_____
_____
_____
_____
_____
_____
_____

LEGACY

This is what I want to be remembered for:

_____

_____

_____

_____

_____

_____

_____

_____

_____

_____

_____

_____

_____

_____

_____

_____

_____

_____

www.ingramcontent.com/pod-product-compliance
Lightning Source LLC
Chambersburg PA
CBHW050247010526
44107CB00003B/226